Careers in
DNA Analysis

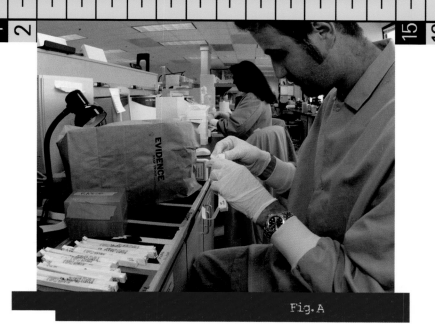

Fig. A

Sarah Sawyer

rosen publishing's
rosen central

New York

Published in 2008 by The Rosen Publishing Group, Inc.
29 East 21st Street, New York, NY 10010

Library of Congress Cataloging-in-Publication Data

Sawyer, Sarah.
Careers in DNA analysis / Sarah Sawyer.—1st ed.
    p. cm.—(Careers in forensics)
Includes bibliographical references and index.
ISBN-13: 978-1-4042-1343-2 (library binding)
1. Forensic sciences—Vocational guidance—Juvenile literature. 2. Criminal investigation—Vocational guidance—Juvenile literature. 3. DNA fingerprinting—Juvenile literature. I. Title.
HV8073.S26 2008
363.25'62—dc22

                                                              2007033924

Manufactured in the United States of America

On the cover: Analysis of DNA.

Contents

If you watch television, you have probably seen some programming related to crime scene investigation (CSI) in both crime dramas and documentaries. Any number of current television shows center on investigative team members who are half scientific genius and half Sherlock Holmes. Within a single broadcast hour, they solve the most complicated and mystifying crimes with the help of genetic material and other clues and trace evidence (such as fingerprints, bodily fluids, and gunpowder residue) left at the scene of the crime.

Perhaps you have watched some of these shows season after season, have gotten to know the characters, and have been intrigued by their personalities, relationships, and the adventurous lives they lead. Maybe you have even begun to consider a career in criminal forensics, which is the use of science to help solve crimes. Do you find yourself watching the news and wishing you were involved in solving crimes within your community? Are you interested in finding the most efficient, accurate, and fair ways to solve crimes and see that victims and their families receive justice as soon as

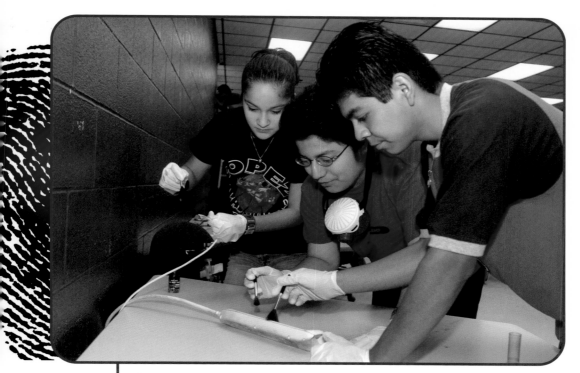

Members of a high school law enforcement academy gather fingerprints. Early hands-on experience in criminal forensics will help test your passion and ability for this career choice.

possible? Maybe you have started thinking you would like to become a forensic scientist someday and—like the exciting characters you see on television—detect genetic materials on evidence found at crime scenes and analyze it for DNA matches with criminals or their victims. Maybe you find the idea of testifying in court about DNA matches exciting. Perhaps you have even started to daydream of having a career working within the specialized criminal forensics field of DNA fingerprinting, and that's why you have opened this book.

If so, good for you! You've taken a great first step toward evaluating and planning for your future career. Reading all about a career before you commit years of work to it is a great idea because there are things you can do today—even before you graduate from high school—that would help you create a career for yourself like the ones you daydream about.

In these pages you will find background information, job descriptions, education plans, job search tips, and career advice that will help you make an educated choice about whether criminal DNA analysis is the career field for you. If this information leads you to conclude that, as much as you enjoy watching *CSI* on television and imagining yourself as one of the crackerjack scientists on the show, your interest in the work portrayed in the stories ends when the episode does, then you will still have gained valuable insight from this book. It is this kind of research and educated consideration that will help you choose the career path that will make you happiest in your adult life.

DNA Analysis

DNA is the genetic material that contains the blueprint for every living thing. Every living thing made up of cells has DNA, and every living thing's DNA is unique and at least slightly different from all others'.

These days, DNA provides us with more information than what a living thing will look like, how it will behave, and how it will grow and develop. Now, it can actually provide a kind of "fingerprint" that will help solve crimes and mysteries. If someone goes missing in a mall parking lot and a blood stain is found nearby, forensics investigators can analyze the DNA present in that blood and see if it matches the DNA found in the hair taken from the hairbrush of the missing person. If the two sets of DNA match, the investigators can reasonably conclude that the missing person met with foul play of some kind. Similarly, if the DNA of skin cells found under the fingernails of a strangled murder victim matches that of a suspect, the evidence against him or her would be considerably stronger. A convincing case for his or her guilt could be made in court.

DNA Fingerprinting in the Real World

David Caruso as Lt. Horatio Caine in the popular CBS drama *CSI: Miami*. Shows like this are where many people get their information regarding DNA fingerprinting.

On television, a detective uses a gloved hand to pick up some personal item from a crime scene—an article of clothing, a paper coffee cup, a strand of hair, or perhaps a half-smoked, lipstick-streaked cigarette in an ashtray—places it in a plastic baggie, drops it off with a friend at the forensics lab, and has genetic tests run that definitively link it to a suspect as soon as the commercial break is over. That is a highly fictional representation of a very real criminal forensics technique: DNA fingerprinting.

It is possible to take a strand of hair, a sample of saliva, or some other type of bodily fluid or substance, extract its DNA, analyze its distinctive DNA pattern, and associate it with a specific person. It is just that in the real world, the process is a bit more complicated and a lot slower than depicted on television.

Television makes the process of convicting someone based on DNA evidence look as easy as picking up a stray hair, looking at it under a microscope, and running the crime lab equivalent of a Google search. But, of course, the real-life process is much more complicated than that. In this chapter, we will walk though the basic techniques involved in mapping a DNA fingerprint, giving you a much more realistic idea of what goes on in a DNA forensics lab on a day-to-day basis.

DNA Basics

In order to get an accurate picture of what DNA analysis is like, you will need to know a little something about DNA. "DNA" is short for deoxyribonucleic acid. It is the microscopic genetic material located in the nucleus of every cell, and it defines the way these cells will grow and work together to form a whole organism— plant or animal. DNA is literally what makes you . . . you.

Every cell of an organism has the exact same sequence of DNA stored in each of its cells. And, with the exception of identical twins, every organism has DNA that is completely unique to it and different from any other member of its species. DNA is what makes it possible for every person to be a unique individual.

You can quickly tell one person from another by just looking at them and comparing, but it would not be as easy to tell one person's strand of DNA from another person's DNA. That is because certain sections of DNA are the same from species to species. All frogs share some parts of their DNA but show differences in other parts or sequences. The same goes for hamsters, dogs, and, of course, people.

A strand of human DNA is made up of forty-two chromosomes. Thirty-two thousand genes can be found within those forty-two chromosomes. Each of those 32,000 genes is made up of a long series in which one of four chemicals is matched in sets of two. These paired sets of two chemicals are called base pairs. It is the patterns of base pairs that differ from gene to gene and that make us all unique. It is the unique order in which these base pairs are found—their patterning—that makes a distinctive, one-of-a-kind DNA fingerprint.

The educational show *Newton's Apple* offers a basic explanation of the unique nature of each person's DNA and how this can allow for genetic fingerprinting:

A DNA molecule resembles a long, twisted ladder. The supports of the ladder are the same for everyone, but the rungs are what make us all different. Each rung is made of a pair of organic molecules called nitrogen bases—adenine, thymine, cytosine, and guanine—usually symbolized as A, T, C, and G. The sequence of the rungs is important. The bases constitute a code for different proteins, much like the letters of an alphabet form words and sentences. Certain areas of the DNA molecule have no currently understood function,

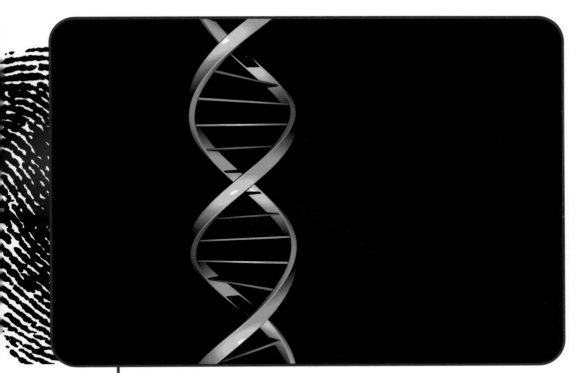

This is the double helix configuration characteristic of a DNA molecule. It resembles a twisting ladder with supports and rungs. It is these "rungs" and their sequence that are entirely unique in each individual.

but they appear to vary widely among individuals. The most common form of DNA profiling, abbreviated RFLP, is a way of showing the unique patterns of bases in some of these areas.

Only some sections of DNA are the same for each member of a species. Other sections will contain differences, and it is these differences that make creatures unique from other members of their species. It is also these different sections that make it possible

DNA Goes to Great Lengths

The Centre for Integrated Genomics in British Columbia reports that if our strands of DNA were stretched out in a straight line, the forty-six chromosomes that make up the human genome would extend more than six feet (close to two meters). A genome is an organism's entire hereditary information, which is encoded in its DNA. If the length of the 100 trillion cells contained within each human being could be stretched out in a straight line, it would traverse more than 113 billion miles (182 billion kilometers), enough material to travel to the sun and back 610 times.

to determine what specific individual left a trace of DNA at a crime scene. DNA, like a fingerprint, is particular to the individual who leaves traces of it behind. No one else's DNA would match it.

The work of the DNA analyst is to take the DNA apart, photograph it, and then compare it to other samples in order to identify a suspect or victim. That is what DNA analysts do all day and every day. It is impossible to understand what they do without understanding the process, so let's take a moment to learn more about DNA analysis itself.

DNA Evidence Collection

Unlike what you often see on television, evidence is rarely collected from the crime scene by the same person who will do the DNA analysis. Detectives and crime scene investigators (CSIs) gather evidence, forensic scientists analyze it, and the two groups do not overlap.

The CSI must be careful to avoid cross-contamination by accidentally mixing two or more

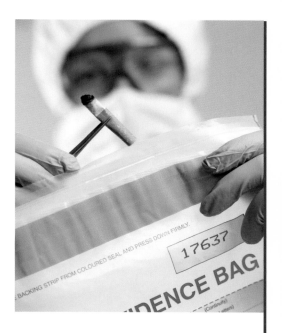

A forensics officer uses tiny forceps to place a cigarette butt into an evidence bag.

samples of DNA from two or more individuals. For example, there may be multiple blood stains from several sources. Each stain must be sampled, labeled, and stored separately. DNA can be surprisingly durable. It can often be recovered from stains that have set for days, or from fabrics that have been long immersed in water, or from bones buried years earlier. In general, however, at least 100 cells must be present in the substance to be examined in order for a full and accurate DNA analysis to be conducted.

Once delivered to the lab, evidence is labeled again, documented, and stored by the lab's "receiving" professional until the DNA analyst is ready to work. There may be quite a gap between the time the information is gathered and the time it is taken to the lab.

How DNA Is Analyzed

The two most popular ways in which DNA might be examined are restriction fragment length polymorphism (RFLP) and polymerase chain reaction (PCR). RFLP relies on an enzyme (a protein chemical) to digest some of the DNA and break it into fragments known as sequences. Scientists call these breaking points endonuclease recognition sites. PCR is a technique that allows scientists to isolate and greatly amplify (expand or enlarge) a fragment or particular sequence of interest of DNA. Analysts then zero in on the specific DNA fragments that demonstrate unique patterns of base pairs, patterns that no two individuals share.

The basic process a forensic analyst follows to examine and identify DNA begins with the taking of sample cells from a person whose DNA needs to be analyzed. One method would be to swab the inside of someone's cheek to collect a few inner membrane cells to use as a sample. It is easy to do and does not hurt the subject one bit. Other sources of cell samples include the blood, semen, hair, and other bodily fluids and tissues taken from the victim or found at the crime scene.

Shirley Harris, of the Georgia Bureau of Investigation, loads DNA samples from inmates into an analyzer in her crime lab.

Sample cells are easily transferred from the cotton swab (or other collection device) into a test tube. Some of those cells would then be spun in a micro-centrifuge, a device that uses a powerful spinning action to separate the cells from any liquid or other materials contained in the sample. Once separated, the liquid is removed so that only the skin cells remain. The cells are added to a mix of chemicals that buffers cells and digests unneeded proteins that are present in them. The tube containing the cells is put in a coolish waterbath, then floated in boiling water.

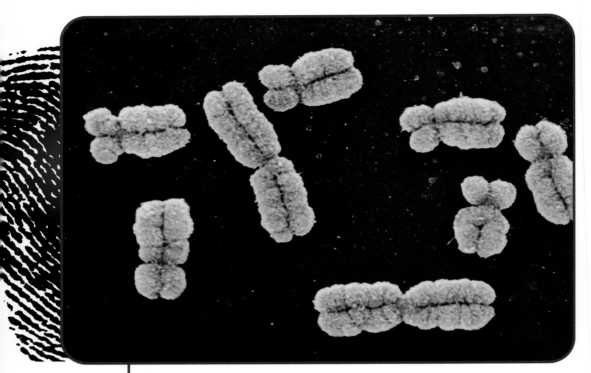

This is a color-enhanced scanning electron micrograph of a human chromosome.

After the temperature treatments, the cells are put in the micro-centrifuge again so that DNA is spun to the top of the tube and can be found in the supernate—or top layer—of liquid. This process gets the DNA out of the nucleus of the cell, isolating it so that it can be analyzed for fingerprinting.

Now that the DNA is isolated, it is broken down even further using a technique known as gel electrophoresis. The "gel" is an agarose mixture made from agar, the same seaweed that is used to make gelatin. It is mixed with some other chemicals and put into a tray made of UV (ultraviolet) transparent plastic. The mixture is microwaved to make sure all the chemicals melt to a pure liquid state. It is then taken out of the microwave, and a tool known as a sample comb is placed in the tray. The scientists wait for the gel to solidify with the comb inside.

Once the agarose gel is solid, the comb is removed, and the microscopic DNA sample mixed with buffering liquid is poured in its place. Electrodes are attached to the tray, and they send waves of electricity flowing through the agarose gel and through the DNA sample. When this happens, the DNA scatters and then re-sorts itself. It is injected with ethidium bromide, a fluorescent dye that makes the DNA visible.

Next, the whole tray is covered with a nylon sheet and soaked overnight. This transfers the DNA material to the nylon, which will act as a sort of microscope slide, allowing the DNA to be viewed and analyzed. But before that can happen, a little more sorting of the DNA is required. Radioactive probes are added to the nylon sheet. They attach themselves to the DNA sequences that are not needed for the creation of a DNA fingerprint. The radioactive probes and the extra, unnecessary genetic material are washed off the nylon sheet, leaving just the one-of-a-kind DNA material that generates the DNA fingerprint remaining on the sheet. The resulting distinctive pattern is transferred from the nylon to X-ray film and developed. A photo of a DNA fingerprint has now been created.

This geneticist examines an autoradiogram showing the genetic sequence of nucleotide bases in one strand of DNA.

These florescent prints are entered into and read by a computer called a DNA sequencer. This process creates a chart called a chromatogram. The chromatogram can be used to make a host of comparisons and contrasts to another DNA sample. In this way, DNA taken from skin cells found under a victim's fingernails can be "fingerprinted" and compared with the DNA "fingerprint" generated from cells sampled from a prime suspect. If the chromatogram reveals similarities or identical patterns, the case is one step closer to being solved. It would appear that the victim scratched the skin of the suspect in a life-or-death struggle before being murdered.

Chapter

2

Real-Life DNA Analysts at Work

Did you notice that in the prior description of DNA fingerprinting techniques there is no mention of forensic analysts going to the crime scene, talking with suspects and victims, reenacting the crime, or doing any of the detective work that the characters on *CSI* do? It's because in the real world, that sort of thing is simply not part of the DNA analysts' job description. Detective work is literally "not their job."

A DNA Analyst's Job Description

The Orange County Forensics Science Services describes the workings of its DNA lab in this way:

- Location, characterization, and DNA profiling of blood, semen, and other physiological materials
- Searching for DNA profiles on items of evidence that were worn or handled by perpetrators and victims

- Comparison of DNA profiles within and between cases locally and submission of eligible profiles to the state and national CODIS DNA databases for searching to link and solve crimes
- Parentage determination for criminal cases

From this list, you can see that working as a DNA analyst means just that—analyzing the DNA of victims and suspects. It happens in the lab with the help of lab equipment. It does not happen in interrogation rooms or out on the beat in the middle of the night or in a hail of gunfire. It happens mostly during business hours, and it does not happen quickly.

Lt. Jim Pierson, director of the Michigan State Police's Grand Rapids forensics lab, told Sally Barber of the *Cadillac News*, "The [CSI] portrayals [on television] are based on fact, but some of the things are unrealistic as far as what the public can truly expect from forensic scientists." For example, Lt. Pierson pointed out that evidence analysis can take up to six months in real life, a far cry from the instant answers seen on television.

Daily Life in a Real DNA Lab

Another difference between the daily work of an actual DNA analyst and one portrayed on television is the equipment used. What you see on television is often state-of-the-art or even experimental technology. In reality, state and local forensics labs often do not

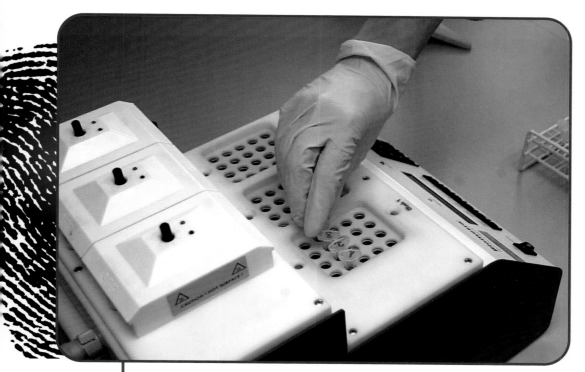

Technology, like this machine used to spin and separate DNA for analysis, is costly and always changing. Many forensics labs—and the professionals that work in them—work hard to keep current.

have enough money to purchase every new piece of equipment on the market or to train their people in the latest technologies.

Philip Cheasley worked in a DNA lab in London, England (the birthplace of DNA analysis), and described it this way in an interview with *Science* magazine: "Although [the job] sounds exciting, the day-to-day work can be quite repetitive, since it is basically the same routine of preparing countless, anonymous profiles." He also mentioned that he was trained for the possibility of being called as a witness in a trial to explain or defend his findings. "Despite

Getting Real About CSI

Gina Steward, a thirty-nine-year-old CSI, was asked by Susan Young of the *Oakland Tribune* to describe the difference between what she sees in CSI shows and what she knows from her real-life career as a CSI in California. She replied, "You can't get DNA results in a day, much less in a minute. It might take us about three days to get the results. You have to do extraction, spinning, and a lot of waiting. It also depends on what kind of DNA you are working with. Skin cells take longer than other DNA. And when you do send a fingerprint to be searched, the computer doesn't pop up with a photo and history of the person. You get a list of candidates to narrow the search."

being on-call several times," he said, "I was disappointed not to have been called to give evidence. Although certainly nerve-racking, it would have been really interesting to be involved in a trial."

While Cheasley was not called into trial, many DNA analysts are. Dana Soderholm, a CSI working for the Kansas Bureau of Investigation, has been called in to testify with regard to evidence in criminal cases. She occasionally discusses cases with the media also, but she describes her job as taking place mostly in the lab.

In this demonstration, tape on a backer card is used to "lift," or capture, a fingerprint.

As the mother of a young daughter, she appreciates that the job's hours are fairly predictable and that she is not likely to be called away to a crime scene in the middle of the night. Her workday does include reading notes on a case and the occasional presentation of evidence. Most of her time, however, is spent processing scientific data and interpreting and documenting the results.

Now that you know a little more about the daily work of someone in a DNA lab, have your career aspirations changed? Are you disappointed that there is less "cops and robbers"–style work? Or, are you relived that you will not be exposed to that level of violence? Do you think you have the scientific, painstaking, and meticulous mind-set and natural talents that are necessary to enjoy and excel in a job like this? If so, you may be well on your way. The next step for you will be preparing for the training and education that you will need to succeed as a DNA analyst.

Chapter

3

Laying the Educational Groundwork in High School

Nearly all DNA analysis jobs in crime laboratories—including entry-level positions—require at least a four-year bachelor's degree in biology, chemistry, or forensic science. During your university years, you will need to acquire a solid grounding in the sciences by taking high-level courses in molecular biology, statistics, genetics, biochemistry, organic chemistry, laboratory techniques and procedures, and the various forensic sciences.

If you are in high school now, what kind of educational path should you plan and pursue? Will a college degree in biology, chemistry, or mathematics be the most useful foundation for a career in DNA analysis? Will you need to take language courses? Will you have to enroll in special law enforcement or legal courses? There are many questions to ask, but the best way to get the information you need is to go to an organization that knows the answers. The American Academy of Forensic Sciences (AFFS) has a "Young Forensic Scientists' Forum" that is an excellent source of information for those wishing to

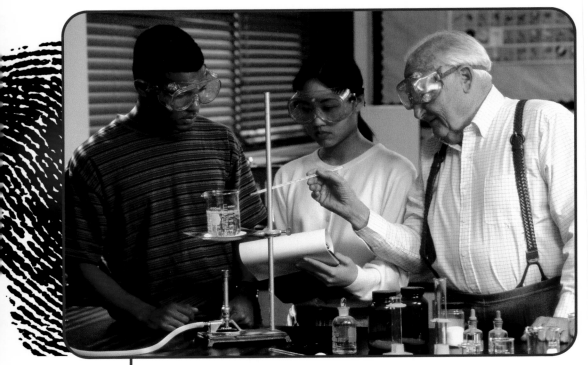

The science you learn in school today may be what makes it possible for you to successfully take on a caseload as a DNA analyst later in life.

learn more about careers in forensic science and how to get the necessary education for good jobs in the field.

High School and College Coursework

According to the AFFS, a minimum of a bachelor's degree in a science such as chemistry, biology, or physics is required for good laboratory jobs in criminal forensics. Regardless of your major, your coursework should include microscopy, statistics, and lab work. But the AFFS also recommends that students interested in criminal forensics do not wait till college to begin laying the groundwork for an eventual career in the field.

While still in high school, students can begin focusing on establishing a strong background in math and science by taking all the biology, chemistry, and physics classes that are offered. You can also take higher-level courses at your local community college. Since forensic scientists write a lot of reports and provide expert testimony during criminal trials, make sure you take writing and public-speaking courses as well.

Taking the appropriate math and science courses while still in high school can help you determine if you will be good at, interested in, and enjoy your college coursework and future career. Do math, biology, and chemistry come easily to you? Are they things that you are good at but require some extra work on your part? Or, are they subjects in which you struggle to pass? Do not be afraid to answer these questions honestly. The answers you come up with do not determine whether or not you will have the career of your dreams. They will simply help you to identify your strengths and weaknesses and provide you with a realistic sense of how much you will need to work in certain areas in order to get where you want to go.

Your answers may also help you discover whether your abilities and interests truly match up with your career goals, and if you have fastened upon a career path that is not suitable for you or which

Active participation in your own education means asking questions, listening attentively to answers, and making the most of your time in school. These are skills that will serve you well as a criminal forensic scientist.

you have romanticized. A career in DNA analysis requires many years of hard and often tedious work. Be sure you know the daily reality of what you are getting into and what skills and personal qualities the career demands.

If you think that the subjects you would need to take will be too hard for you, do not throw in the towel just yet. It may be that your skills do not mesh well with those required in DNA analysis. But it may also be the case that improving your study skills, time management, and goal-setting practices will greatly improve your aptitude and abilities. To help figure all this out, speak to an honest and trusted teacher or guidance counselor at your school. He or she may be able to help you develop the skills you need to better succeed, or steer you into a career path that is more likely to suit your talents and bring you lasting professional happiness and satisfaction.

Regular consultations with your school guidance counselor will help you stay on track in the pursuit of the career of your dreams.

Getting Involved in Criminal Forensics Right Now

You are not the only young person excited about forensic science. There are lots of young people just like you who are intrigued and inspired by *CSI*-type shows and, as a result, are considering a career in criminal forensics. Teachers love it when kids get excited about science. They will often capitalize on their students' excitement to create an opportunity for unique educational experiences and further

Camp CSI

Arkansas State University offered a CSI Camp for upper-level high school students in 2006. The camp provided hands-on experience at reconstructed crime scenes, in working laboratories, and in the classroom. Crime scene processing, lab analysis (forensic biology and chemistry), investigative strategies, and psychological profiling were all covered. Lecturers included ASU faculty, law enforcement personnel, professional investigators, and laboratory scientists. High school senior Brad Hughes found the experience to be invaluable. Hughes was quoted on Arkansas State University's Web site as saying: "The CSI camp at ASU is awesome. I met some really neat people, and I am excited to attend the advanced camp this summer. The camp helped me decide that crime scene investigation is the career I want to pursue."

Hughes has got the right idea in putting his enthusiasm for criminal forensics to the test in practical, real-world situations. Discovering ways to engage in forensic science firsthand, rather than relying on false impressions gathered from television shows, will give you a much clearer idea of whether or not this is a field of study that is truly suited to you and in which you will be happy and successful.

The best way to know if you would enjoy working in laboratories and conducting scientific research is to try your hand at it while you are still a student.

learning. This is one reason why CSI camps are suddenly popping up all over the country.

Some of these are actual sleepover camps held at a campground or on a college campus during the summer. Others are offered as optional after-school or community education programs. Different camps are tailored to different age levels, but they all share the same goal: teaching the basics of forensic science to people like you who want to learn them and are just beginning to explore an interest in this branch of criminal science.

Will one of these camps get you a job as a forensic scientist? No. You will not learn all that you need to know to get the job you want or be able to perform its tasks. But you might learn enough to know whether or not DNA fingerprinting is an area you would really like to work in.

College Education, Training, and Jobs

A great way to map out the educational path that you will need to follow to become a DNA analyst is to read the want ads. Even though you are several years and about 120 college credits away from your first job, it is nevertheless a good idea to read job listings for your career of choice. Not only do they clearly spell out the educational requirements for each job; they also provide information about the kind of work you will be doing on a daily basis.

Entry-Level Position

The following job listing, based on an actual employment advertisement, describes an entry-level position in the DNA research and identification laboratory of a private company that maintains a criminal offender database:

> Jones Technology is seeking applicants for the position of DNA Analyst-in-Training. This position is available with the convicted offender data banking team at the DNA research and identification laboratory located in

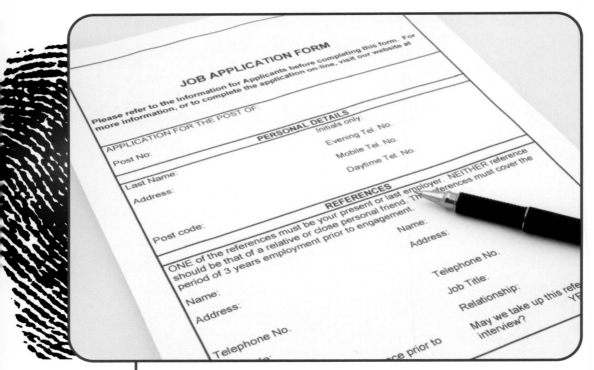

Even though you are probably not ready to apply for a professional position today, it is not too soon to take a peek at a job application or "help wanted" ad. Looking over one will give you an idea of what qualities potential employers would like in a candidate.

North Jersey. Qualifications include a minimum of a bachelor's degree in molecular biology, genetics, or similar life science, which includes completion of genetics, molecular biology, statistics, and biochemistry. Unofficial transcripts are required.

This is the type of position you will most likely obtain immediately after college. It offers invaluable, on-the-job training that will help you get a higher-level laboratory job after a year or two. The job requires a "minimum of a bachelor's degree in molecular biology, genetics, or similar life sciences." That means in order to get this entry-level job, you will need to have a four-year degree from an accredited college in one of these subjects. The ad also points out that a qualified applicant will have successfully passed classes in genetics, molecular biology, statistics, and biochemistry during his or her degree program. Proof of a degree and the appropriate coursework will have to be presented in the form of transcripts—a record of the classes you took and the grades you received—from your college.

The job listing does not provide much detail about the nature of the work, but it is clear that the laboratory analyzes and records the DNA of criminal offenders—people who have committed crimes. This personal genetic data is entered into a database, presumably for use by police departments and federal investigators. Chances are that the analyst-in-training, in addition to performing some basic lab work, would also be responsible for data entry, which is inputting the genetic information into the computerized database.

DNA Analyst Position

After you spend a year or two in an entry-level job like this one, gradually acquiring more laboratory experience and technical skills, it will be time for you to seek your next position. It could be within the lab or company you are currently working for, or elsewhere. Your next position in the field of DNA analysis may be something like the one listed in the following excerpted job advertisement that's based on an actual job listing:

DNA LABORATORY ANALYST III

The Mercer County Medical Examiner's Office is seeking applicants for the position of DNA Laboratory Analyst III. Qualifications include a bachelor's degree in biology, chemistry, forensic science, or related fields. Must have successful completion of coursework in biochemistry, molecular biology, and genetics, along with coursework or training that covers the subject areas of statistics and/or population genetics. One year of experience in a forensic laboratory is preferred.

As with the first job listing, this one clearly spells out the minimum requirements necessary for an applicant to be considered for the job. The educational requirements are basically the same: a bachelor's degree in biology, chemistry, or forensic science, with successfully completed coursework in biochemistry, molecular biology, genetics, and statistics. The real difference between the two positions' minimum requirements is the level of experience necessary. The position of DNA laboratory analyst III is not an entry-level job. It requires at least a year of hands-on, professional, forensic lab experience.

This job posting goes on to list the kinds of forensic knowledge and lab experience and techniques the applicant will be expected to have. Only some of this knowledge and experience could be gained in academic study; previous work experience in a lab would be the only way to acquire much of it. This list of requirements also offers some insight into the kinds of tasks you would be performing daily:

Jobs in forensic sciences require—and offer—extensive experience working in labs.

Knowledge of forensic DNA principles, laboratory techniques, and technology; knowledge of polymerase chain reaction (PCR), short tandem repeat (STR) analysis, and capillary electrophoresis methods; knowledge of biological evidence collection and preservation techniques; knowledge of rules of evidence; knowledge of forensic serology, basic human anatomy/physiology, and laboratory safety; experience with evidence screening, DNA extraction, quantification, polymerase chain reaction, and amplification of short tandem repeat fragments.

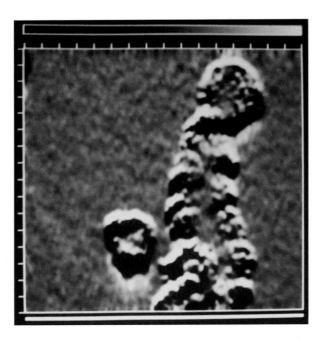

An unaltered length of DNA has been photographed using a scanning tunneling microscope.

A polymerase chain reaction is a technique used to isolate and amplify a section of DNA, allowing lab analysts to identify genetic fingerprints. Short tandem repeat refers to repeating patterns of nucleotides (the chemical compounds that are the structural units of DNA) on adjacent sequences of an individual's DNA. The analysis of these repeating patterns helps researchers create a unique genetic profile for the person whose DNA is being examined. Capillary electrophoresis is a technique that separates and organizes DNA molecules by size, facilitating the process of genetic analysis and DNA sequencing (mapping). Forensic serology is the study and identification of the type and characteristics of blood, blood testing, and bloodstain examination. It also involves the analysis of semen, saliva, sweat, and other bodily fluids that may be found at a crime scene.

In addition to spelling out for you what you need to know how to do in order to get this job, the employment listing also reveals the kind of work you will be doing if you indeed land the job—serious, nuts-and-bolts lab work in which you will be isolating, sequencing, and analyzing DNA through a variety of biochemical techniques, as well as performing other criminal forensics tasks, such as blood-stain identification and analysis. The employment listing provides even more information about the job's duties:

Under the direction of the Forensic Biology Director, the employee will perform scientific examination and analysis of biological evidence collected in connection with death and criminal investigations. Testing may include screening for the presence of biological fluids and DNA analysis using PCR/STR based methods. Findings are presented in a technical report and verbally in a court of law through expert witness testimony. . . Works with laboratory chemicals and various biological fluids—may be exposed to blood-borne pathogens.

This portion of the listing explicitly states that you would be working on cases involving deaths deemed to be suspicious or criminal in nature. Part of your job would be fluid and DNA testing to help determine the identities of both the victim (if unknown) and the attacker. It points out that your job would involve not only lab work but also report writing and providing expert testimony on your findings in a court of law. The person hired for this job must demonstrate writing ability, attention to detail, clarity, comprehensibility, and a high comfort level speaking in front of a group. The advertisement issues a warning of sorts: You will be exposed to other people's blood and other bodily fluids, and the risk of infection is very real. This can be a dangerous and gruesome job, and it is not for the faint of heart or weak of stomach.

The job listing goes on to request complete college transcripts and notifies applicants that a criminal background check is required. Since the lab analyst will be working in a government office that supports law enforcement efforts and deals with highly personal and confidential materials, a candidate for the job must have a clean record that reveals no history of criminal activity or poor judgment, such as drug use, theft, fraud, or blackmail. The job listing ends with a salary range of $40,000 to $60,000. The exact salary that you will ultimately be offered will be based upon your level of education and experience.

Managerial Lab Position

After several years spent performing the nitty-gritty investigative and analytical work in a criminal forensics lab, you may decide you want to spend less time handling blood and other bodily fluids, hunching over a microscope, and conducting complex biochemical tests and procedures in order to isolate, analyze, and identify the DNA of suspects and victims. You may be tired of working under a boss and may want to become the boss yourself: a lab manager or "technical leader."

This upward shift would take you away from much of the basic lab work and would free you up to oversee lab operations, manage a staff, write and review case reports, and provide expert testimony and opinions. It would also result in a significant bump in salary, more perks, and greater prestige. But with greater prestige comes stricter requirements and more responsibilities. Consider the following job listing (again based on an actual employment advertisement):

DNA LAB TECHNICAL LEADER

The Dane County Sheriff's Office is seeking applicants for the position of DNA Lab Technical Leader. This position will direct the design, development, validation, and implementation of a new forensic DNA Laboratory. The successful candidate will be required to perform the duties of a DNA Lab Technical Leader and be responsible for creating and maintaining required accreditations, as well as Quality Assurance Standards (QAS) for Forensic DNA Laboratories. Hence, the applicant must possess an earned master's degree from an accredited academic institution; or the equivalent in a biological, chemical, or forensic science with earned credits in genetics, biochemistry, and molecular biology or other subjects that provide a basic understanding of the foundation of forensic DNA analysis, as well as statistics and/or population genetics as it applies to forensic DNA analysis. This position performs administrative tasks and supervises the operation and development of the Crime Laboratory, including personnel and equipment. Job responsibilities include conducting training for appropriate individuals or groups; testifying in court as to the laboratory findings; reviewing work of other analysts; performing proficiency tests and other quality assurance duties; participating in continuing education programs; collecting, documenting, and preserving evidence; and maintaining laboratory instruments. Applicants must have exceptional communication skills (written and verbal), with the ability to generate and explain detailed scientific reports. Two (2) years supervisory experience in a crime laboratory is preferred.

As you can see, this job is primarily managerial. It offers the applicant the unique opportunity of overseeing the design and development of a brand-new forensics DNA lab. Once the lab is built and operational, the technical leader will supervise all operations, equipment, and personnel (employees). Rather than doing the hands-on lab work, the technical leader will be more involved in the training, monitoring, and evaluating of employees, ensuring that safety and quality standards are upheld and equipment maintained, and providing expert testimony in court regarding DNA evidence found at a crime scene. Because this is a higher-level job, with more experience required and greater responsibilities demanded, the candidate must have at least a master's degree in biological, chemical, or forensic science, and have successfully completed the relevant coursework.

Yet, just because you may be moving up into a more managerial role within the DNA lab, this does not mean that a background in forensic lab techniques and procedures is no longer so important or that you will not be required to perform nitty-gritty evidence analysis again. In order to adequately train, supervise, and evaluate your employees, you must have a thorough, expert, and up-to-date knowledge of lab work, an ability to perform it, and a talent for teaching it to others who possess less knowledge and experience than you. In addition, certain cases, usually of a high-profile nature, may require your hands-on involvement in the lab. For these reasons, the job listing stresses the crucial importance of lab proficiency in a candidate:

Highly desirable qualifications include knowledge of handling forensic evidence; knowledge of the principles and practices of quantitative/qualitative organic chemistry; knowledge of basic laboratory techniques and procedures; experience in short tandem repeat (STR) analysis; and experience working with forensic DNA using capillary electrophoresis. With limited supervision, the candidate will conduct physical, microscopic, immunological, and biochemical analyses on evidence submitted, and provide written reports based on the analyst's interpretation of results providing expert testimony in federal, state, and local courts.

Once a DNA lab analyst, always a DNA lab analyst. When considering a career in DNA analysis or another area of criminal forensics, be sure that lab work is your first love. Because no matter how high you may rise in your profession, chances are you will always be called upon, at least once in a while, to roll up your sleeves and perform some basic, down-and-dirty examination of fluids and by-the-numbers DNA analysis.

DNA Lab Jobs Without a College Degree

If some of the DNA analysis jobs discussed above sound interesting to you, but for one reason or another college is not in your immediate future, there might still be a way for you to work in the forensic sciences. Or, maybe you would prefer to try working in a lab first and see how you like it and how good you are at it before you invest an enormous amount of time, energy, and money into getting the education you would need to secure a good, career-building job within the field.

If this is the case, you might consider applying for a different, lower-level job within the lab. This would give you exposure to DNA

FBI unit chief Dawn Herkenham holds a chart of the CODIS Architecture and describes how DNA samples taken from convicted felons may help solve otherwise unsolvable crimes and "cold cases."

analysis but wouldn't require so much educational and professional preparation. Some jobs, such as lab technician or evidence cataloguer, do not always require a bachelor's degree. A recent job listing in North Carolina for a DNA specimen accessioner/data entry operator required only a high school diploma. The job, for a company that uses DNA analysis to establish paternity (determining who the father of a child is) would involve receiving and opening specimen containers (containing some substance from which

DNA can be recovered and isolated, such as hair, skin, blood, or semen); labeling specimens accurately and appropriately; using a computer database to match the specimen with the associated parties involved in the case (the child, mother, and suspected father); accurately entering data associated with the case into the computer database; and fulfilling other clerical duties, such as filing, photocopying, typing, letter writing, and telephone answering.

You would not perform actual lab work or DNA analysis, but you would witness it firsthand and work alongside DNA analysts. In your time there, you would have plenty of opportunities to learn about the nature of lab work and speak to analysts and ask them about the requirements, challenges, tedium, joys, and rewards of their work. You would then be in a much better position to make an educated decision about whether or not DNA analysis is for you and if you should commit yourself to years of education and training.

Getting Information, Taking Stock

Take a moment to review your own education in light of what you have learned about what potential employers will want from you. Are you qualified for any of these jobs right now? Will you be soon? What relevant high school classes have you taken? Do you have a high school diploma yet, or will you earn one soon? Do you want to put your interest in DNA analysis and criminal forensics to the test by getting a low-level data-entry job or an unpaid internship in a lab before committing yourself to a course of college study and a career path?

If you are sure that you want to study criminal forensics in college, have you taken any AP (advanced placement) math or science courses that you think might help get you into a college that has a good biology, chemistry, or forensic science program and prepare you to work in a job like the ones you have just read about? Once you have identified what kind of job within DNA analysis you would like to pursue, consider your answers to these questions and use them to map out your educational plan and employment strategy.

5 | Alternative and Future Careers in DNA Analysis

There are many different kinds of jobs available within the field of DNA analysis, sequencing, and fingerprinting. Some are related to criminal justice, while others are concerned with human health or pure biological research. There are jobs available in big cities and smaller towns, in county medical examiners' offices, local police departments, federal investigative agencies, and multi-million-dollar private biotechnology companies. There are jobs in which you would analyze DNA in order to establish paternity, identify and combat genetic diseases, compare the human genetic composition with that of other mammal species, or bioengineer more plentiful and hardy crops.

Staying Current

A great way to become familiar with the wide range of employment possibilities associated with DNA analysis, both inside and outside the field of criminal forensics, is to register with an online job-posting site like Monster.com, CareerBuilder.com, or Yahoo! Jobs and ask to have

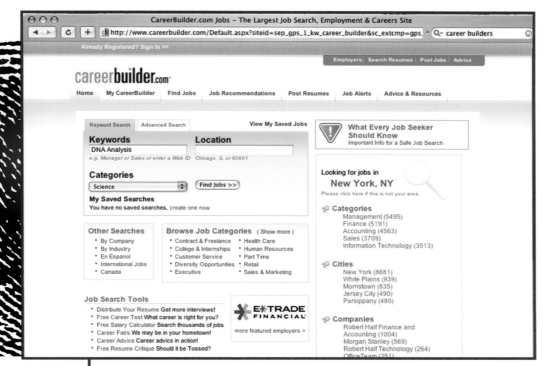

Inside the browser window:

http://www.careerbuilder.com/Default.aspx?siteid=sep_gps_1_kw_career_builder&sc_extcmp=gps. ^ career builders

Already Registered? Sign In >>

Employers: Search Resumes | Post Jobs | Advice

careerbuilder.com

Home   My CareerBuilder   Find Jobs   Job Recommendations   Post Resumes   Job Alerts   Advice & Resources

Keyword Search   Advanced Search   View My Saved Jobs

Keywords   **Location**
DNA Analysis
e.g. Manager or Sales or enter a Web ID   Chicago, IL or 60601

Categories
Science   (Find Jobs >>)

My Saved Searches
You have no saved searches, create one now

Other Searches   **Browse Job Categories** (Show more)
* By Company   * Contract & Freelance   * Health Care
* By Industry   * College & Internships   * Human Resources
* En Espanol   * Customer Service   * Part Time
* International Jobs   * Diversity Opportunities * Retail
* Canada   * Executive   * Sales & Marketing

Job Search Tools
* Distribute Your Resume **Get more interviews!**
* Free Career Test **What career is right for you?**   **E✳TRADE**
* Free Salary Calculator **Search thousands of jobs**   **FINANCIAL**
* Career Fairs **We may be in your hometown!**
* Career Advice **Career advice in action!**   more featured employers >
* Free Resume Critique **Should it be Tossed?**

⚠ **What Every Job Seeker Should Know**
Important Info for a Safe Job Search

Looking for jobs in
New York, NY
Please click here if this is not your area.

Categories
    Management (5495)
    Finance (5191)
    Accounting (4563)
    Sales (3709)
    Information Technology (3513)

Cities
    New York (8681)
    White Plains (939)
    Morristown (835)
    Jersey City (490)
    Parsippany (480)

Companies
    Robert Half Finance and
    Accounting (1004)
    Morgan Stanley (569)
    Robert Half Technology (264)
    OfficeTeam (251)

Studying job posting Web sites like CareerBuilder.com will help you stay current in an ever-changing job market and keep you informed about technological advances in your career of choice.

postings that feature the key words "DNA fingerprinting," "forensic science," "DNA analysis," "DNA sequencing," or "genetic" e-mailed to you.

Although you may not be applying for these jobs for several years yet, there's nothing wrong with reading the posts. They will give you a clearer picture of what those hiring for your future dream job are looking for. Especially in rapidly evolving high-technology fields like forensic science, it is important to stay current on job

A computer scans and records a fingerprint taken from a person's fingertip that is pressed against a screen.

skill requirements. During the time that you are in school, the field will undoubtedly change, perhaps dramatically. Keeping a casual eye on job postings will help you make sure that you are taking the courses and getting the work experience you need to be a competitive applicant when you are ready to look for a job, even if that time is still a ways off.

A Wide and Rapidly Expanding Field

As you read job postings sent to you by online employment sites, it will become clear that working as a CSI is not the only job available to someone possessing DNA analysis skills. DNA finger-printing is more of a skill set than a family of careers, so it is likely that elements of your job will remain constant, even if you change laboratories or companies. The techniques of DNA analysis will not change job to job, but the reason for performing the analysis will. Criminal investigation is not the only reason one might turn to DNA fingerprinting. It is also used to determine the biological parents of a baby (when parentage is in doubt or disputed), to identify unidentified dead bodies, to confirm whether or not babies were accidentally switched at a hospital, to identify an individual's susceptibility to a genetic disease, and a myriad of other reasons.

As the practice of DNA analysis grows and develops, new categories of jobs will emerge. Perhaps you are interested in fine-tuning the process of DNA fingerprinting. In that case, you might want to work in forensic research and development. Perhaps at some point in your career you will want to share the information you have gathered with others. If so, a teaching career in one of the many forensic science programs cropping up in colleges across the country might be perfect for you.

Maybe you will become interested in helping people live healthier lives. You could turn your study of DNA and its properties to medical applications. The world of genetics, genetic testing, and genetic medicine is growing quickly. The future is bound to hold many varied and lucrative positions helping people make the most of this new science.

Go to the Source for Information and Advice

Researching all the employment possibilities available to a DNA analyst is time well spent. Watching job boards and postings will help you see the broader employment picture, too. But perhaps the best way to find out more information about your options is to go straight to the source. Contact someone working in DNA analysis and ask him or her for an informational interview.

The goal of an informational interview is to learn more about a job that interests you. Informational interviews are not about you trying to get a job offer from the person you speak with. Instead,

Take advantage of career days and job fairs at school. Working professionals will always be your best source of accurate information about your career of choice, and they may provide you with valuable contacts.

you are simply trying to gather more information about your field of interest in order to determine if it is truly right for you, and, if so, how you should go about building a career in that field. You are doing the interviewing in this case; you are not being interviewed for a job.

Your career or guidance counselor at school might be able to set you up on an informational interview with someone who works in DNA analysis. During this interview you should ask the person what his or her career is like; what a typical day is like; what advice he or she has for an interested student like yourself; and what other jobs outside of criminal forensics someone with DNA analysis experience might be able to pursue.

If you inform your teachers of your interest, keep up with your schoolwork, and continue to use the employment research techniques explored in this book, you will be well positioned to succeed in your future career in DNA analysis.

centrifuge A machine that separates materials out of a mixture by spinning the mixture at a very high speed.

chromosome A strand of DNA that carries all of the hereditary information that is necessary to generate life.

criminal offender A person convicted of a crime.

CSI A crime scene investigator. Also the name of a television series based on fictionalized portrayals of such investigators.

DNA Deoxyribonucleic acid. The unique genetic code contained in every cell of every living thing.

DNA fingerprint The unique pattern of DNA that identifies a sample as belonging to a particular individual.

DNA sequencer A computer created to read and compare strands of DNA.

entry-level position A job well-suited for someone who is inexperienced and new to a career and/or just out of college or high school.

ethidium bromide A fluorescent dye used to make microscopic items, like strands of DNA, easier to see.

forensic science The application of scientific principles, techniques, and procedures to the solving of crimes.

gel electrophoresis A process that uses a gel base and an electric current to sort pieces of DNA, making them ready to read as a fingerprint.

genome The total genetic content of an organism.

nucleus A cell's center, where all the DNA material is located.

transcripts Records of grades and classes for a particular student issued by the school he or she attends or attended.

American Academy of Forensic Sciences

410 North 21st Street

Colorado Springs, CO 80904

(719) 636-1100

Web site: http://www.aafs.org

A nonprofit professional society established in 1948 and devoted to the improvement, administration, and achievement of justice through the application of science to the processes of law.

American Society of Crime Laboratory Directors, Inc.

139K Technology Drive

Garner, NC 27529

(919) 773-2044

Web site: http://www.ascld.org

The American Society of Crime Laboratory Directors is a nonprofit professional society of crime laboratory directors and forensic science managers dedicated to promoting excellence in forensic science through leadership and innovation.

Association of Certified Forensic Investigators of Canada

173 Homewood Avenue

Willowdale, ON M2M 1K4

Canada

(416) 226-3018 or (877) 552-5585

Web site: http://www.acfi.ca

The Association of Certified Forensic Investigators is a nonprofit Canadian organization whose objective is to foster a national forum and governing body for the affiliation of professionals who provide their expertise in the areas of fraud prevention, detection, and investigation.

California Criminalistics Institute

4949 Broadway, Room A104

Sacramento, CA 95820

Web site: http://www.cci.ca.gov

The California Criminalistics Institute, a unit of the California Department of Justice, Bureau of Forensic Services, provides specialized forensic science training to personnel who are practitioners in the field.

Canadian Society of Forensic Science

3332 McCarthy Road

P.O. Box 37040

Ottawa, ON K1V 0W0

Canada

Web site: http://ww2.csfs.ca

This nonprofit organization seeks to maintain professional standards and promote the study and enhance the stature of forensic science.

Federal Bureau of Investigation

J. Edgar Hoover Building

935 Pennsylvania Avenue NW

Washington, DC 20535-0001

(202) 324-3000

Web site: http://www.fbi.gov

The FBI's mission is to protect and defend the United States against terrorist and foreign intelligence threats, uphold and enforce the criminal laws of the United States, and provide leadership and criminal justice services to federal, state, municipal, and international agencies and partners.

National Forensic Science Technology Center

7881 114th Avenue North

Largo, FL 33773

(727) 549-6067

Web site: http://www.nfstc.org

The National Forensic Science Technology Center is a not-for-profit corporation funded by a Cooperative Agreement with the National Institute of Justice and provides programs that build individual competency and quality systems for the forensic science community in the United States.

Web Sites

Due to the changing nature of Internet links, Rosen Publishing has developed an online list of Web sites related to the subject of this book. The site is updated regularly. Please use this link to access the list:

http://www.rosenlinks.com/cif/dnan

For Further Reading

Adelman, Howard C., M.D. *Forensic Medicine*. New York, NY: Chelsea House, 2006.

Baden, Michael M., and Marion Roach. *Dead Reckoning: The New Science of Catching Killers*. New York, NY: Simon & Schuster, 2001.

Ball, Jacqueline A. *Forensics*. Milwaukee, WI: Gareth Stevens Publishing, 2003.

Bell, Suzanne, Ph.D. *The Facts On File Dictionary of Forensic Science*. New York, NY: Checkmark Books, 2004.

Camenson, Blythe. *Opportunities in Forensic Science Careers*. Chicago, IL: McGraw-Hill, 2001.

Genge, Ngaire E. *The Forensic Casebook: The Science of Crime Scene Investigation*. New York, NY: The Ballantine Publishing Group, 2002.

Lyle, Douglas P. *Forensics for Dummies*. New York, NY: Hungry Minds, 2004.

Pentland, Peter, and Pennie Stoyles. *Forensic Science*. New York, NY: Chelsea House Publishers, 2002.

Platt, Richard. *Crime Scene: The Ultimate Guide to Forensic Science*. New York, NY: Reed Business Information, 2003.

Ramsland, Katherine M. *Forensic Science of CSI*. New York, NY: Berkley Books, 2001.

Saferston R. *Criminalistics: An Introduction to Forensic Science*. 7th ed. Upper Saddie River, NJ: Prentice Hall, 2001.

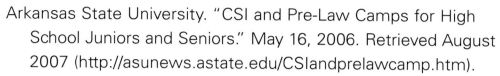

Bibliography

Arkansas State University. "CSI and Pre-Law Camps for High School Juniors and Seniors." May 16, 2006. Retrieved August 2007 (http://asunews.astate.edu/CSIandprelawcamp.htm).

Colorado State University. "Agarose Gel Electrophoresis of DNA." January 2000. Retrieved August 2007 (http://arbl.cvmbs. colostate.edu/hbooks/genetics/biotech/gels/agardna.html).

Massachusetts Institute of Technology. "Recombinant DNA Methods." Retrieved August 2007 (http://web.mit.edu/7.02/ virtual_lab/RDM/RDM1virtuallab.html).

Newton's Apple. "DNA Fingerprinting." Retrieved August 2007 (http://www.reachoutmichigan.org/funexperiments/agesubject/ lessons/newton/dna.html).

Young, Susan. "CSI: (Not) as Seen on TV," *Oakland Tribune*. July 4, 2005, p.1, sec. 1.

About the Author

Sarah Sawyer is a writer with a passion for career development. When she's not writing educational or lifestyle pieces, she's networking, learning to network, teaching career development workshops, and trying to help connect people with the information they need to make their dreams a reality. She has been a David Caruso fan since *NYPD Blue* and is now a devoted *CSI* fan. She learned a lot writing this book and is excited to share it.

Photo Credits

Cover © Getty Images; p. 5 © Bob Daemmrich/Photo Edit; p. 8 © CBA via Getty Images; p. 11 © Shutterstock; pp. 13, 18 © Tek Images/Photo Researchers; pp. 15, 21, 23, 31, 38, 45 AP Photo; p. 16 © Biophoto Associates/Photo Researchers; pp. 26, 50 © David Young-Wolff/Photo Edit; p. 28 © Dana White/Photo Edit; p. 29 © Michelle D. Bridwell/Photo Edit; p. 34 © www.istockphoto.com; p. 37 © www.istockphoto/Andrei Tchernov; p. 53 © www.istockphoto.com/Lisa F. Young.

Designer: Les Kanturek; **Photo Researcher:** Marty Levick